EDINBURGH

AN ILLUSTRATED JOURNEY

Doug Corrance (photographs) is based in Edinburgh. He has photographed several books on Scotland along with travel guides on everywhere from India and Japan to New York and the Côte d'Azur. He began his career on a local paper in the Scottish Highlands, and after spells in London and Sydney spent 11 years as staff photographer with the Scottish Tourist Board.

Karen Fitzpatrick (text) has worked in book publishing for many years, some of which she spent in London. She now lives in her native Scotland with her husband and works as an editor and writer. Her particular areas of interest include Scottish culture and literature.

This is a FLAME TREE Book
Created for LOMOND

FLAME TREE PUBLISHING
Crabtree Hall, Crabtree Lane
Fulham, London SW6 6TY
www.flametreepublishing.com

Flame Tree is part of The Foundry Creative Media Company Limited

Copyright © 2005 Flame Tree Publishing

05 07 09 08 06
1 3 5 7 9 10 8 6 4 2

ISBN 1 842040804

Printed in China

Thanks to: Frances Bodiam, Sarah Goulding, Chris Herbert, Julia Rolf, Melinda Révész, Claire Walker, Nick Wells and Polly Willis

EDINBURGH

AN ILLUSTRATED JOURNEY

PHOTOGRAPHS: DOUGLAS CORRANCE

TEXT: KAREN FITZPATRICK

LOMOND

CONTENTS

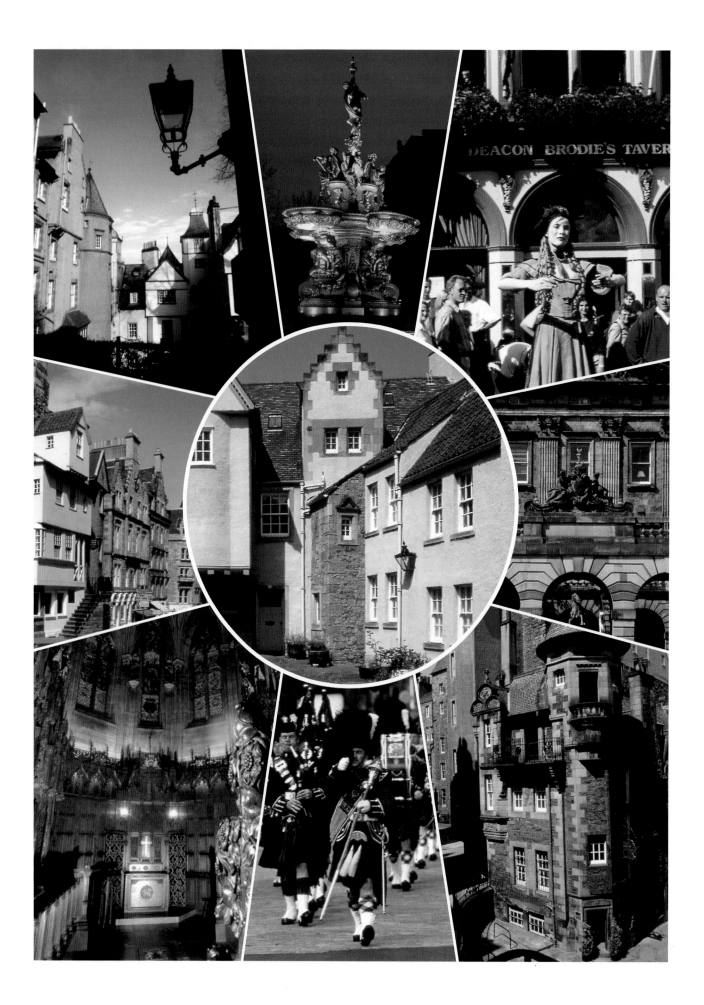

THE ROYAL MILE

Believed to be the oldest street in Edinburgh, the Royal Mile extends 1 mile and 107 yards from the castle in the west to the gates of the Palace of Holyroodhouse in the east. Running down the shoulder of the hill from the castle to its esplanade, the Royal Mile comprises a number of connected streets starting with Castlehill, then Lawnmarket, High Street, Canongate and Abbey Street. As described by the writer Daniel Defoe, it is the "largest, longest and finest street in the world" and provides a fascinating insight into the city's history and, indeed, Scotland itself.

THE ROYAL MILE

Edinburgh's historic high street is alive with history. During its long existence, it has been home to kings, queens, princes, knights, murderers, thieves, beggars, hangmen and market-traders. Although these people have all but vanished, their echoes can still be heard in its closes and quiet corners.

PROCESSION, ROYAL MILE

One of the highlights of the Edinburgh Festival – and one of its most gloriously Scottish traditions – is the Military Tattoo, which takes place on the castle esplanade and celebrates the culture and history of Scotland. The various Scottish regiments, together with guest regiments from around the world, wear full uniform and gather in a procession, accompanied by the sound of bagpipes and drums. At the end of the show, a lone piper plays from the castle ramparts in a truly moving finale.

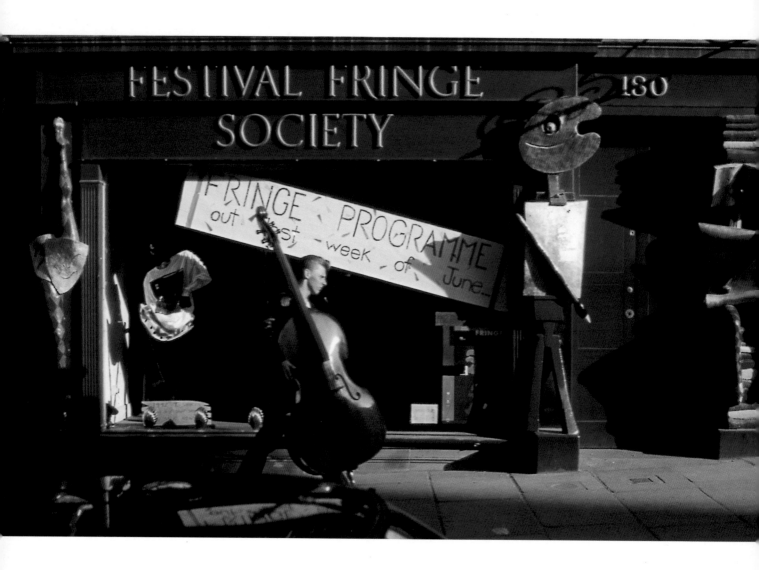

EDINBURGH FESTIVAL FRINGE

August is the month of all things 'fringe', when Scotland's capital city erupts into a riotous, bustling cornucopia of creativity. The vastness of entertainment on offer is unrivalled anywhere else on the globe. Since its inception in 1947, it continues to strive to encompass new and experimental acts, to push the boundaries and accommodate everyone who wants to attend. The Scotsman, rightly so, describes it as "one of the artistic wonders of the world".

HOGMANAY

Every year, Edinburgh opens its streets to revellers and hosts what it proudly claims to be Britain's best New Year's Eve party. Hogmanay is more than just another name for New Year's Eve – it is a national festival that is celebrated by the Scots in a style that has to be seen to be believed. The street party is centred around Princes Street Gardens, and usually features live music by some of Britain's top acts. The highlight of the celebrations is the firework display, framed by the backdrop of Edinburgh Castle, which begins at the stroke of midnight.

EDINBURGH CASTLE

By night (previous page), from the west (above), late afternoon (opposite).
Rising from an ancient volcanic plug, Edinburgh Castle (shown here
and on the previous page) looms over the capital city from a height
of 80 m (262 ft). A majestic sight to behold, it is the city's biggest
tourist attraction; it dominates the skyline just as it has dominated
Edinburgh's long and complex history. The castle's variety of
architectural styles demonstrate both its history and its service
as a stronghold and seat of kings. Housed in the castle is the
famous Stone of Destiny, seized by the English and taken to
Westminster Abbey in 1296. It only returned to Scotland in 1996.

ST MARGARET'S CHAPEL, EDINBURGH CASTLE

This tiny Norman Chapel is dedicated to St Margaret, the wife of
King Malcolm III, and was built c. 1110 in her honour, perhaps by
her youngest son, King David I. It is the smallest and oldest chapel
in Edinburgh, measuring 5 × 3 m (16 × 10 ft). Having survived
the many sackings of the castle, the chapel is still in use today and
members of the castle garrison have the right to be married in it.

THE HONOURS OF SCOTLAND, EDINBURGH CASTLE

The Honours of Scotland consist of a crown, sceptre and sword that
are on display alongside the Stone of Destiny in Edinburgh Castle. They
were used in the coronations of the infant Mary, Queen of Scots in
1543, James VI in 1567, Charles I in 1633 and the last Scots coronation:
that of Charles II at Scone in 1651. Fearful that the regalia might fall
into the hands of Oliver Cromwell, the 'Honours' were hidden until
the restoration of the monarchy in 1660, and were then used at the
sittings of Scottish Parliament until the Treaty of Union in 1707. Made
redundant, they were stored away until 1818 when Sir Walter Scott
scoured the castle and found them locked away in a wooden chest.
They have remained on display ever since.

MILITARY TATTOO

A huge success with locals and international tourists alike, the Military Tattoo commands an audience of approximately 217,000 each year and boasts performers from over 30 countries worldwide. The evening begins with the phenomenal marching of Scottish soldiers across the

drawbridge to the esplanade, booming out tunes such as 'The Skye Boat Song' and 'The Garb of Old Gaul'. Throughout the evening, home-grown talent and international guests enthral the audience. The night is rounded off with spectacular fireworks and a skin-tingling recital of 'Auld Lang Syne'.

SCOTS GUARD

Formed in 1642 by King Charles I, the original role of the Scots Guards was to protect Scottish settlers in Ulster. Over the years they have fought in most major British wars, including the American Revolution (1775–83), the South African War (1861–64), both First and Second World Wars (1914–18, 1939–45) and the First Gulf War (1991). The Band of the Scots Guard are experienced entertainers at the Military Tattoo and are popular the world over. In 1998 they undertook a 10-week tour of the US and Canada, and in 2000 they toured Australia and took part in the first performance of the Edinburgh Tattoo abroad in New Zealand.

Statue of Field Marshal Haig

Douglas Haig was born in Edinburgh on 19 June 1861. He fought
in the South African War and the First World War, and became a
commander-in-chief in 1915. It was his attack on the Hindenburg Line
in 1918 that brought about the end of the war. (He has been criticised,
however, for the high number of casualties while he was in charge.)
In 1919 he became an Earl and by 1921 he had founded the British
Legion charity. He died on 29 January 1928. The bronze equestrian
statue of him on the Esplanade at Edinburgh Castle was donated in
his memory by the Bombay parsee, Sir Dhumjibhoy Bomanzi.

ONE O'CLOCK GUN

The One O'Clock Gun, one of the Edinburgh's most famous attractions, was established in 1861. The gun is fired every day, except Sundays, Good Friday and Christmas Day, at one o'clock – the exception is Hogmanay when it fires at midnight to welcome in the New Year. The original purpose of the gun was to allow boats on the Firth of Forth to set their clocks to the right time, but nowadays it functions as a tourist attraction, managing to startle many an unsuspecting visitor. The One O'Clock Gun has its own exhibition at Edinburgh Castle.

MONS MEG

This six-ton siege gun was given to James II in 1457 by Philip the Good, Duke of Burgundy. It was made in Mons in Belgium and was used in action against the English at the siege of Norham Castle in 1497. In 1540 the gun was deemed useful for ceremonial purposes only; it was used in 1558 to celebrate the marriage of Mary, Queen of Scots to the French Dauphin François. In 1681 the gun blew up and was stored at the Tower of London until 1829, when it was returned to Edinburgh Castle. It is now on display in front of St Margaret's Chapel.

RAMSAY GARDEN

At the summit of Princes Street Gardens, and adjoining the castle esplanade, lies Ramsay Garden, with its unsurpassable views of the city. A prestigious group of tenement houses, with their bright colours and picturesque turrets and gables, they were built between 1892 and 1894. Designed by the Edinburgh visionary Patrick Geddes (along with Sydney Mitchell), these apartments, situated next to Edinburgh Castle, were built in keeping with Edinburgh's history and culture and provided green outlooks and modern amenities. Originally created for Edinburgh University intellectuals, they are now amongst the most sought-after properties in Edinburgh.

CAMERA OBSCURA

Originally a seventeenth-century tenement housing block, the Camera
Obscura and Outlook Tower is Edinburgh's oldest attraction. Operating
since the 1850s, the Camera Obscura (located in the hexagonal tower
of the Outlook Tower) captures live moving pictures of the city of
Edinburgh – visitors can seemingly touch cars and buses, and enjoy
the voyeuristic view of unwitting passers-by. A guide is also present
and tells Edinburgh's story as well as pointing out its historic buildings.
Other points of interest in the Outlook Tower are the 3-D Hologram
Display, the 360° views from the rooftop terrace, the Superscope
Telescope and the Magic Gallery.

LADY STAIR'S HOUSE (THE WRITERS' MUSEUM)

Just off the Lawnmarket is Lady Stair's House (1622), named after
the widow of John Dalrymple, the 1st Earl of Stair, who lived there
between 1719 and 1759. In 1893 the house was bought by Archibald
Primrose, the 5th Earl of Rosebery, who gave it to the citizens
of Edinburgh in 1907. It now functions as a writers' museum and is
dedicated to three of Scotland's most illustrious scribes: Robert Burns,
Sir Walter Scott and Robert Louis Stevenson.

GLADSTONE'S LAND (INTERIOR)

A fine example of a seventeenth-century 'high rise', Gladstone's Land is the most important example of this type of housing still surviving in Edinburgh. The six-storey merchant house was completed in 1620 and was the home of the Edinburgh burgess Thomas Gledstanes, who filled it with fine paintings and furnishings of the period. The remarkable painted ceilings are of particular note. The house features a mock shop-booth with replica goods on the ground floor, and on the first floor there is a reconstructed Edinburgh home, typical of the period. The house is owned by the National Trust for Scotland.

DEACON BRODIE'S TAVERN

The inspiration for Robert Louis Stevenson's novel *The Strange Case of Dr Jeckyll and Mr Hyde* (1886), Deacon Brodie (1741–88) was a cabinet-maker and respected city official by day and a notorious robber by night, with an appetite for drinking, gambling and womanising. On his last raid – of the excise office in Chessels Court – he was caught and sentenced to hang. This tavern, established in 1806, lies close to Brodie's place of execution (where he was hanged in 1788) and pays tribute to his legendary villainous status.

HIGH KIRK OF ST GILES

The only parish church of medieval Edinburgh, the High Kirk of St Giles is considered the 'home of Presbyterianism', and it was from here that the preacher John Knox ignited the Scottish Reformation. Parts of the original medieval building can still be seen, such as the late fifteenth-century crowned tower and the four massive octagonal pillars that support the central tower, which supposedly date back to the earlier Norman church of 1120. The Pre-Raphaelite windows and the memorial window to Robert Burns are magnificent, as well as the intricate ornamentation and carvings.

THISTLE CHAPEL, HIGH KIRK OF ST GILES

The Thistle Chapel was built between 1909 and 1911 by Robert Lorimer and is the chapel of the Knights of the Order of the Thistle, Scotland's foremost Order of Chivalry. The Order was established by James VII in 1687 and consisted of the monarch and 16 knights. The chapel is small and splendid, opulent and extravagant, with carved and painted fittings of incredible detail that pay homage to the skill of Edinburgh men William and Alexander Crow. Look closely to find an angel playing the bagpipes.

PARLIAMENT SQUARE

The square was created in the early nineteenth century and is built on the kirkyard of St Giles, where religious reformer John Knox lies buried. Its elegance is primarily owed to the neo-classical Law Courts, dating from the eighteenth century. The square is dominated by Parliament House, which housed the Scottish Parliament until the Act of Union in 1707, and the impressive High Kirk of St Giles. The square also features the Mercat Cross and the statue of King Charles II; next to it is the Heart of Midlothian, which is emblazoned on the cobbled street.

THE HEART OF MIDLOTHIAN

A reminder of the city's grim past, this heart-shape of cobblestones represents the fifteenth-century Tolbooth, which operated as the town prison and site of many public executions – it was here that the Duke of Montrose was executed in 1650 and his head put on display. The Tolbooth was nicknamed the 'Heart of Midlothian' and it features in Sir Walter Scott's novel of the same name. Criminals used to spit on the doors of the Tolbooth as they walked by, a tradition still carried out by locals today on the spot that marks its site.

CITY CHAMBERS

Designed by John Adam and located halfway down the Royal Mile, Edinburgh's City Chambers stand proud, an indication of the city's burgeoning wealth in the eighteenth century. Built in 1761 as the Royal Exchange (at a cost of £31,000), it was unpopular with the city traders who preferred to do business on the street. By the early nineteenth century it was functioning as the city council's headquarters. Mary King's Close (reputedly the most haunted place in the city) runs beneath the Chambers.

TRON KIRK

On the corner of the High Street and South Bridge, the Tron Kirk is a Grade A listed building and famous Edinburgh landmark. Built between 1637 and 1647 by John Milne, the church features a fine hammer-beam roof and an unusual mix of Gothic and Palladian styles.

The original wooden spire burned down in 1824 in the Great Fire and was replaced with a taller spire by R & R Dickson in 1828. The Tron Kirk closed as a church in 1952 and is now a visitor information centre. The remains of Marlin's Wynd, a sixteenth-century Edinburgh street discovered beneath the church, have been exposed for all to see.

GILLESPIE PLAQUE

This plaque on 231 High Street is dedicated to James Gillespie of Spylaw, an eighteenth-century merchant, who with his brother John established a small snuff empire in the city of Edinburgh. On his death in 1797 he left his estate of £40,000 to the city and instructed that a charitable home be opened for the elderly as well as a free school to educate poor boys. Nowadays, the school is a semi-private establishment, far from what Gillespie had in mind.

JOHN KNOX'S HOUSE

This fifteenth-century house has remained largely unaltered since the 1550s when the Mosman family, who were goldsmiths to Mary, Queen of Scots, lived there. It rises to three storeys and is the most picturesque on the High Street. Outside it features a sundial of Moses pointing to the sun, a water well and a set of forestairs. Many doubt that the famous Protestant reformer John Knox ever lived there, but if he did, it would have been between 1561 and 1572. The interior of the house is highly decorated and has some fine hand-painted ceilings. The house is now run by the Church of Scotland and functions as a museum, where relics of Knox and the Reformation are exhibited.

MUSEUM OF CHILDHOOD

The Museum of Childhood on High Street is frequently described as "the noisiest museum in the world", and with the numbers of children – and parents – who pass through, this is hardly surprising. The museum opened its doors in 1955, the brainchild of Edinburgh councillor Patrick Murray, and was the first in the world to specialise in the history of childhood. Stuffed full with toys, comics, games, 'penny arcade' machines and childhood memorabilia, this museum celebrates the joy of childhood and its cultural significance.

CANONGATE KIRK

Built in 1668 by James Smith for a congregation that had been expelled from a church of the old Holyrood Abbey, King James VII (II of England) decided to turn it into a royal chapel. The church is surprisingly Roman Catholic in style, with a chancel and transepts. Buried in the churchyard are many notable figures, such as Adam Smith, the poet Robert Ferguson and Agnes McLehose, Burns's Clarinda. Canongate Kirk is the parish church of Holyroodhouse and Edinburgh Castle, and the Royal Family regularly worship here when in Edinburgh.

WHITE HORSE CLOSE

Although far from authentic, White Horse Close is one of the most charming closes in the Old Town. It is believed to have originally been used as palace stables, and earned its name from Mary, Queen of Scots' favourite mount. From the seventeenth century an inn on the site functioned as a coach terminus for journeys between Scotland's capital and London. In 1889 the close was rebuilt entirely as workers' houses, and again between 1961 and 1964 in the particular Scots style of Frank Mears & Partners.

THE MUSEUM OF EDINBURGH

Huntly House is home to the Museum of Edinburgh and dates from the sixteenth century, although it was extended in both the seventeenth and eighteenth centuries. The City Corporation opened the building as a museum in 1932 and it functions as the city's principal museum of local history. It is much more than a local museum, however, as there are many items exhibited which are of national importance. The most treasured, perhaps, is the National Covenant, signed in Greyfriars Kirkyard in 1638.

SCOTTISH PARLIAMENT BUILDING

Swathed in controversy, the subject of the Scottish Parliament building is never short of debate — whether it is on the streets of Scotland or in the Debating Chamber itself. This is hardly surprising, when the building's final cost was a staggering £431 million, instead of the original £50 million estimate. Nevertheless, this striking Enric Miralles building signifies the rebirth of a nation. As the Queen said in her speech on the official opening of Parliament on 9 October 2004, it is "a landmark of twenty-first century democracy".

THE PALACE OF HOLYROODHOUSE

The Palace of Holyroodhouse is the official residence of Her Majesty the Queen in Scotland. At the edge of Holyrood Park, it is located at the eastern end of the Royal Mile descending from Edinburgh Castle. Little of the original building remains today – the palace was seriously damaged by the invasion of the Earl of Hertford in 1544 and, later, by Cromwell in 1650. The building that we recognise today is credited to the reconstruction of the palace, which was undertaken by architect Sir William Bruce and builder Robert Mylne for Charles II in 1671.

HOLYROOD ABBEY

Adjacent to the Palace of Holyroodhouse are the ruins of Holyrood Abbey. According to legend, King David I encountered a vicious stag on the site in 1128, and when he grabbed its antlers it disappeared, leaving a crucifix in his hands. In acknowledgement of the miracle, the king founded the Monastery of the Holy Rood. The monastery flourished into a splendid and important abbey, but it suffered greatly during the Reformation and again during the 1688 revolution. Although some restoration work was attempted during the eighteenth century, the roof collapsed in 1768 and the abbey continues to dilapidate.

SOUTHERN EDINBURGH

Often overlooked by those unaware of what lies beyond the crowded Royal Mile, the streets that make up southern Edinburgh are filled with wonderful surprises. The different architectural styles are revealed in the form of period houses, museums and galleries, theatres, Edinburgh University's buildings and arts, crafts and antique shops, all unveiling Edinburgh's strong historical background. Intertwined with the city's modern-day life of cafés and bars, and filled with locals, students and tourists, the area makes Edinburgh a city of cultural contrast, in which the old and the new work together.

USHER HALL

With its superb acoustics and seating capacity of 2,900, Usher Hall is Edinburgh's principal concert venue. This octagonal Baroque building, with its copper domed roof and sculptures by Birnie Rhind, Crosland McLure and H. S. Gamley, was built in 1896. In 1911 the foundation stone was laid by King George V and Queen Mary, and by 1914 the venue was open. The hall is one of the city's major venues during the Edinburgh International Festival, and provides world-class and diverse music all year round.

TRAVERSE THEATRE

This began as a tiny theatre in the Lawnmarket area of Edinburgh in 1963, in a building that had previously been a brothel! Its current location is in the rather more cultural Cambridge Street, close to the Usher Hall and Royal Lyceum Theatre. The building itself was built in 1992 and is part of the Saltire Court office complex. The theatre is renowned for its artistic integrity and production of new, contemporary material, and is unique in Scotland in its commitment to new, especially Scottish, writing. During the Edinburgh Festival it regularly receives Fringe Firsts and Herald Angels.

GRASSMARKET

Tucked away behind Edinburgh Castle, the Grassmarket area offers the contrast of charming antique shops and open-air cafes by day, and a bustling variety of bars and clubs by night. Edinburgh's main weekly market functioned here (after being granted a charter in 1477 by James III) until 1911, selling wood and timber, and later horses, cattle and grain. The Grassmarket still has the feel of a medieval market square, and the views of the castle are breathtaking. The area does have a more grisly past, however, as it was once the location of the public gallows and site of public executions.

VICTORIA STREET

Victoria Street often goes unnoticed by visitors to Edinburgh, but it is a must for the more adventurous. Located to the south of the Royal Mile, this street is rich with a variety of shops, often with the most unexpected goods on sale, that mingle proudly amongst an array of period housing. During the eighteenth century this street was one of the most fashionable to live on in Edinburgh, mainly because of the first Assembly Rooms, which were built there in 1710.

GREYFRIARS BOBBY

The companion and watchdog of policeman John Gray, Skye terrier Bobby was constantly at his side during life and death. Gray died from tuberculosis in 1858 and was buried in Greyfriars Kirkyard. Bobby was so devoted to his master that he lay on his grave, leaving only for food, for 14 years until his own death in 1872. The little dog had touched so many people's hearts that a statue was commissioned in his honour by Baroness Angelia Georgina Burdett-Coutts, the President of the Ladies Committee of the RSPCA. It was unveiled in 1873 opposite Greyfriars Kirkyard.

GREYFRIARS KIRKYARD

A host of distinguished Scots lie buried in this graveyard, including architects William Adam and James Craig (designer of the New Town) and the poet Allan Ramsay. The most famous resident of all, however, is Greyfriars Bobby, the Skye terrier who lies approximately 50 yards from his master, John Gray. The kirkyard has a reputation for its stunning collection of seventeenth-century monuments, the finest in Scotland and perhaps one of the best in the UK. The kirk itself holds an important place in Scottish history as the place where the National Covenant was signed in front of the pulpit in 1638.

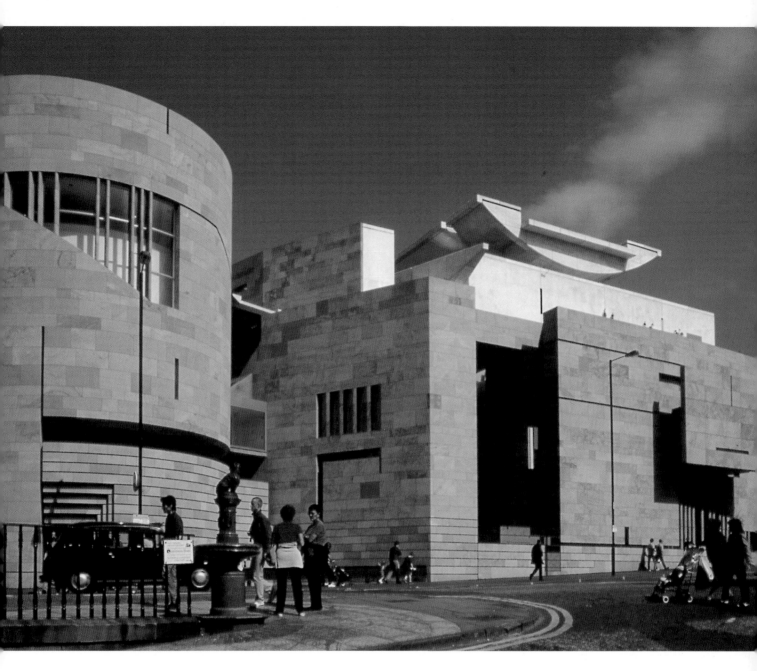

ROYAL MUSEUM OF SCOTLAND

The Victorian building of the Royal Museum of Scotland was designed
by Francis Fowke, a captain of the Royal Engineers. The exterior of the
building is of the Venetian Renaissance style, whereas the inside of the
main hall embraces the design style of the Crystal Palace in London, by
Joseph Paxton. There are 36 galleries consisting of a treasure trove of
exhibits with everything from Islamic Art to a permanent exhibition on
evolution. There is even a blue whale's skeleton suspended from the
ceiling, which has hung in the Mammal Hall for over 100 years.

MUSEUM OF SCOTLAND

Completed in 1998, this impressive building was designed by award-
winning architects Benson & Forsyth. From its roof-top garden can
be seen Edinburgh old and new: its spires, towers, windy medieval
and elegant Georgian streets, right across to the hills beyond the city,
and the sea. Indeed, the architects' inspiration behind their design
was to meld the city's eclectic mixture of building styles and create
a sympathetic surrounding for some of Scotland's greatest treasures.

EDINBURGH INTERNATIONAL FESTIVAL

The embodiment of quality cultural and artistic excellence, the Edinburgh International Festival is, as quoted in The Times, "the envy of the world". Founded in 1947, its aim still remains the same: to offer the most highly acclaimed performances in the world by the best artists in their field. This philosophy has strengthened and gained credibility over the years so that it continues to "enliven and enrich the cultural life of Europe, Britain and Scotland and provide a period of flowering of the human spirit."

FESTIVAL THEATRE

There has been a theatre on the Nicholson Street site of the current Edinburgh Festival Theatre for over 100 years. This striking, glass-fronted structure opened its doors in 1994 and, with one of the biggest stages in Europe, lays on large-scale productions of opera, dance and musicals. The original auditorium of the former Empire Palace Theatre, with its mixture of neo-Classical and Art Nouveau styles, has been preserved. It is believed that the ghost of illusionist the 'Great Lafayette' has haunted the premises since his death in the 1911 fire which destroyed part of the Empire Palace.

TENEMENT HOUSING, MARCHMONT

Tenement housing is often inaccurately associated with slum accommodation and deprivation, and although many tenement flats in Scotland were destroyed because of the terrible living conditions they offered, there are many that were – and continue to be – amongst some of the most sought after and architecturally beautiful buildings in the country. The tenements of Marchmont are a prime example. With their fine Baronial architecture and green, woodland views of the Meadows, they are never on the housing market for very long and are highly desirable amongst Edinburgh's middle classes.

THE MEADOWS

Just a ten-minute walk south of the Royal Mile is the Meadows, a large expanse of wooded parkland that is popular for sports such as football, cricket, tennis, jogging or even just playing frisbee. At one time the park was under water and was called South Loch or Burgh Loch, and provided the city of Edinburgh with its main supply of water. The loch was drained in 1740 and the parkland was developed. It remains very much the same today.

OUR DYNAMIC EARTH

Designed by Sir Michael Hopkins, Our Dynamic Earth is one of the few successes of the Millennium Commission, unlike the Millennium Dome in London, which shares a similar architectural structure. With its smooth curves and taut cables and masts, it stands proudly – a modern architectural giant set against the backdrop of Arthur's Seat and the Salisbury Crags. Inside, the journey of our earth – past, present and future – is split into 11 galleries, where visitors can experience simulated earthquakes and volcanoes, and even the Big Bang.

THE NEW TOWN

Although far from 'new', since most of the New Town stems from the Georgian period, it is nonetheless dramatically different from Edinburgh's ancient Old Town. Exuding an air of regal elegance, the New Town is very formulaic in its planning, where the streets run in straight, symmetrical lines and the houses, churches and public buildings that grace them all work in perfect harmony. The architect that almost single-handedly designed the New Town is James Craig, and his genius is still prevalent today. His plan was that George Street should be the focus of the New Town, but Princes Street has since stolen its crown. With gardens and magnificent views of the castle on one side and a busy shopping thoroughfare on the other, Princes Street is the busiest and best-known street in Edinburgh.

THE NEW TOWN

At the age of only 22, architect James Craig (1744–95) won a competition organised by Edinburgh Town Council to design the city's New Town. His original plan included two grand squares, connected by three parallel streets. The majority of the buildings in this area were built in sandstone from Craigleath Quarry and are neo-Classical in style. The symmetrically-designed New Town was originally intended as a residential area, but now serves as Edinburgh's bustling commercial centre.

ROBERT LOUIS STEVENSON'S HOUSE, HERIOT ROW

In 1857, the Stevenson family moved to 17 Heriot Row in Edinburgh's New Town, an area lived in by the professional classes. Robert Louis Stevenson, best known for his legendary stories *Treasure Island* and *The Strange Case of Dr Jekyll and Mr Hyde*, was six when he moved to the house and did not leave until 1880 when he had aspirations to travel the world. His journey began in France, where he met his wife Fanny Osbourne, and they finally settled in Samoa, where he died in 1894. Outside 17 Heriot Row a brass plaque hangs in his memory.

MORAY PLACE

Designed by James Gillespie Graham and built for the Earl of
Moray between 1824–27, the Georgian Moray Place is the pièce
de résistance of Gillespie's work. Situated about half a mile to the
north of the west end of Princes Street, it is very different from
James Craig's symmetrical, straight streets that are generally associated
with the New Town. Moray Place is a 12-sided block of four-storey
buildings, featuring columned centrepieces and pilasters, exuding
upper-class elegance, sophistication and luxury.

PRINCES STREET

Acclaimed as a shopper's paradise, with the likes of Jenners (opened in 1838) on the fashion menu, Princes Street is the busiest street in Edinburgh. It was not always intended to be a major attraction, however; in the original plans for the New Town, Princes Street was nothing more than a subsidiary road. Nowadays, it has two faces: on the north side lie myriad commercial outlets, whereas on the south side Edinburgh's cultural heritage is on display, with the Princes Street Gardens, the galleries, the Balmoral Hotel and views of the castle and the old town.

CHARLOTTE SQUARE

Charlotte Square, which was intended as the twin of St Andrew's Square, is considered by many to be the finest square in the New Town. Much of its design was undertaken by Robert Adam and even today his style is undeniable, although he died just as work on the project began. On the west side lies West Register House, which was originally St George's Church. Number 6 is the official residence of the First Minister of Scotland, while number 7, the 'Georgian House', is run by the National Trust for Scotland and provides a fascinating insight into upper-class eighteenth-century life.

WEST REGISTER HOUSE

Situated on the west side of Charlotte Square, West Register House is the original St George's Church. Robert Adam designed the building, but the design was changed significantly by Robert Reed during construction to cut costs. Completed in 1811, the church was in use until 1964 when it was taken over by the Scottish Record Office (now the National Archives of Scotland) to store their documents. Exhibitions are held frequently and the Declaration of Arbroath of 1320 is permanently on display.

ST MARY'S EPISCOPAL CATHEDRAL

The largest church built in Scotland since the Reformation, St Mary's Episcopal Cathedral is a prominent and distinctive feature of Edinburgh's skyline. It was built in 1879 by Sir George Gilbert and boasts three beautiful spires, the central one of which reaches 84 m (275 ft). The church was consecrated on 29 October 1879 and daily services have been held there ever since. Its spacious interior is filled with fine decorative details, but it is the high altar, especially when drenched in coloured light from the stained glass windows, that is the focus of the church.

ST JOHN'S KIRK

Work on this impressive church at the end of Princes Street began
in 1816, and a mere two years later the building was completed and
consecrated (at a cost of £18,000). The perpendicular Gothic style
was decided upon by the designer William Burn. His plan of seven
bays with five windows on each side was altered on construction, and
the building instead features eight bays with six windows on each side.
The church is visited regularly by worshippers as well as sightseers.

ST CUTHBERT'S KIRK

Also known as the West Kirk, St Cuthbert's has a prime position
below Edinburgh Castle. The present church (constructed between
1892–94) is built upon the site of no less than six earlier churches,
perhaps dating as far back as the eighth century. The interior of the
church is sumptuously furnished and decorated and is notable for its
alabaster and marble pulpit, stained glass windows and painted ceilings.
David and Goliath in stained glass, by Tiffany of New York, is
particularly worth seeing.

IN MEMORY OF

THE REV. DAVID DICKSON D.D.

WHO DIED 28th JULY 1842, IN THE 65th YEAR OF HIS AGE,
AND THE FORTIETH OF HIS MINISTRY IN THIS CHURCH AND PARISH.

PRINCES STREET GARDENS

Built on the site of the Nor' Loch, Princes Street Gardens originally functioned as a private garden for residents on the north side of Princes Street, so that they could enjoy uninterrupted views of the castle and the Old Town. In 1876 the gardens opened as a public park and have been enjoyed by the general public ever since. Within the gardens are many statues and monuments, such as the Scott Monument and the statues of David Livingstone and Allan Ramsay, to name but a few, as well as the Floral Clock and the Ross Bandstand, which plays host to summer concerts.

MEMORIAL TO THE ROYAL SCOTS GREYS

Situated in the west of Princes Street Gardens is this bronze equestrian statue by Birnie Rhind paying tribute to the Royal Scots Greys – the oldest regiment in the British Army, who left Edinburgh to fight in the South African War in 1899. The statue was erected on 16 November 1906 and was unveiled by Lord Rosebery. The roll of honour on the sandstone blocks below the statue commemorates those who lost their lives courageously in battle.

THE MOUND

Before the Nor' Loch was drained, the Mound was created to join the Old Town with the New. Originally not much more than a muddy, earthen walkway, it must have been a somewhat unattractive sight in those days. Nowadays, however, the Mound is one of the most attractive streets in Edinburgh, passing Princes Street Gardens, the National Gallery of Scotland, the Royal Scottish Academy, the New College of the University of Edinburgh and the Assembly Hall of the Church of Scotland.

STATUE OF ALLAN RAMSAY

The Carrara marble statue of the famous poet Allan Ramsay, who inspired the likes of Robert Burns, stands at the junction of Princes Street and the Mound. Ramsay's most highly acclaimed work is *The Gentle Shepherd* (1725), but he is also famous for establishing the first-ever library in Britain. The statue, erected in 1865, was sculpted by Sir John Steell and depicts Ramsay in his nightcap, which was reputedly a fashion statement. The medallion portraits attached to the pedestal represent members of Ramsay's family and descendants.

NATIONAL GALLERY OF SCOTLAND

The National Gallery of Scotland, with its magnificent columned porticoes and elegant exterior, was designed by William Henry Playfair and is located on the Mound between the Old and the New Town. Prince Albert laid the foundation stone in 1850 and nine years later the museum was open to the public. As Scotland's finest gallery, it houses an impressive collection of Renaissance to Post-Impressionist European paintings and sculptures. Van Dyck, Gaugin, Raphael and Rembrandt are only a few of the great names represented here. The finest collection of Scottish paintings in the world is also housed in this gallery.

THE SCOTT MONUMENT

This Gothic monument in Princes Street Gardens rises to 67 m (200 ft) and was built in 1846 in commemoration of Edinburgh's literary son, Sir Walter Scott. Designed by George Meikle Kemp, a self-taught architect who won the project in a competition, the design of the monument is very much influenced by Melrose Abbey. Inside the blackened sandstone structure are 287 steps to the top, where the views of the Edinburgh skyline are stunning. A statue of Scott, by Sir John Steell, stands below the arches of the monument.

BALMORAL HOTEL

The 'grand old lady' of Princes Street, the Balmoral is more than just a hotel; it is also a stunning Edinburgh landmark, with its 59 m (195 ft) clock tower a well-known sight on the Edinburgh skyline. Originally named the North British Hotel (after the rail company by whom it was owned), it first opened in 1902 and was very popular with discerning travellers. The service was so luxurious that a lift could take guests directly from Waverley Station to the hotel. The Balmoral continues to offer the very highest standards in accommodation.

THE FLORAL CLOCK

Located in West Princes Street Gardens, the Floral Clock is situated at the foot of the statue of the famous poet Allan Ramsay, and is one of Edinburgh's most cherished tourist attractions. The clock has told the time to visitors of the park since 1903, and it is believed that it is the oldest floral clock in the world. Covered in a beautiful array of seasonal plants and flowers, it operates all year round. When the clock strikes the hour, a cuckoo in a birdhouse to the left of the clock announces the time.

ST ANDREW'S SQUARE

St Andrew's Square was originally designed as the twin of Charlotte Square and was intended to be home to St Andrew's Church. It was never built here, however, because Sir Laurence Dundas built his Palladian town house on the site instead. Seen above, the mansion was built in 1774 under the watchful eye of Sir William Chambers, who was also the architect for Somerset House in London. Nowadays the square houses some of the most important financial institutions in Europe. Indeed, Sir Laurence Dundas's mansion has been the headquarters of the Royal Bank of Scotland since 1852, and its blue dome with gold, star-shaped coffers makes a visit well worthwhile. In the centre of the square is the Melville Monument, a memorial to Henry Dundas, the first Viscount Melville.

CHURCH OF ST ANDREW & ST GEORGE'S

When Sir Laurence Dundas bought what was intended to be the site of St Andrew's Church, the town's planners were forced to think again. At the east end of George Street, which runs off St Andrew's Square, they found their spot and what is now known as the Church of St Andrew and St George's was built. Opened for worship in 1784, this was the first of many new churches to be built in the New Town area. It was designed by Major Andrew Frazer of the Royal Engineers, who gave it an unusual oval exterior, a theme continued inside with a curving gallery and rounded ceiling.

REGISTER HOUSE

At the north end of the North Bridge, and at the east end of Princes
Street, is the prominently positioned Register House. One of Robert
and John Adam's finest pieces of work, this house has been the integral
cog of Scotland's record-keeping system since 1774. Today, the
amount of records is so huge that a number of different buildings
have been allocated to store them, including West Register House
and New Register House. Exhibitions are held regularly and offer
the opportunity to see the fine domed rotunda.

NORTH BRIDGE

The original North Bridge was designed by architect John Milne, along
with John Adam, and consisted of three stone-work arches, stretching
to 346 m (1,135 ft) long. With the development of Waverley Station
and the railway network came the new bridge, replacing its elder in
1895. It was built by Sir William Arrol and is a magnificent steel
structure, now highly protected as a structure of historical and
architectural interest. The sight of this magnificent bridge is just as
impressive as the views from it.

OLD OBSERVATORY, CALTON HILL

There are two observatories on Calton Hill: the City Observatory of 1818, which is the largest, and the Old Observatory (Observatory House) of 1792, which was designed by James Craig, the architect who also designed the New Town. The Old Observatory is no longer in use, but instead functions as a tourist attraction and provides stunning views of the city of Edinburgh. The City Observatory is still used by the Edinburgh Astronomical Society. It is open to the public and has exhibitions and viewings of the night sky.

WATERLOO BRIDGE

Located to the east of Princes Street and near the foot of Calton Hill, Waterloo Bridge consists of a series of triumphal 15 m (50 ft) arches. Construction began on this impressive Regency structure in 1815. The way in which the bridge was designed aimed to conceal the fact that it was a bridge, and it is only at the arch shown here that its true height is revealed. Waterloo Bridge offers good views of the Port of Leith and Edinburgh city centre.

NATIONAL MONUMENT, CALTON HILL

The National Monument is the oldest structure on Calton Hill.
Based on the Parthenon in Athens, this unfinished Acropolis is an
unmistakable and unique feature of Edinburgh's skyline. The project
to build the National Monument, to commemorate those who lost
their lives in the Napoleonic Wars, began in 1816. The architect
William Playfair was commissioned and work started in 1822, but
due to a shortage of funds, building had to be stopped. The structure
has remained untouched since 1829.

NELSON MONUMENT, CALTON HILL

Nelson Monument was designed by Robert Burn, and was built in
1816 in memory of Admiral Lord Nelson's victory and death at the
Battle of Trafalgar in 1805. The monument is an imitation of Nelson's
telescope – even though it is upturned – and has an interior stairway
of 143 steps that lead to a spectacular 360° view of the city and
across to the Firth of Forth. Another striking feature is the time ball,
which is lowered every day at one o'clock, working in co-ordination
with the One O'Clock Gun at Edinburgh Castle.

SUBURBS AND OUTSKIRTS

On the outskirts of Edinburgh city centre is a vast array of places of natural beauty. Best described as 'Scotland in miniature', there are numerous castles and country houses, and the magnificent Holyrood Park – with its palace, Arthur's Seat and the Salisbury Crags within its boundaries – will quench the thirst of anyone interested in Scottish history. Quaint fishing villages, modern galleries and two of the finest bridges in Britain – if not the world – are just a few of the things that make the suburbs of Edinburgh truly worth visiting. Many more are described in the following pages…

DEAN VILLAGE

Formerly known as the Water of Leith Village, Dean Village was a thriving milling hamlet for more than 800 years, with some 11 mills powered by the river. However, with the rise of the large flour mills in Leith in the nineteenth century, industry began to diminish and for many years it was associated with poverty and decay. Nowadays, the restored workers' cottages, warehouses and mill buildings enhance the village's authenticity. It is also home to the Scottish National Gallery of Modern Art and the Dean Gallery, but its biggest attraction is probably the four-arched Dean Bridge, built in 1832 and designed by Thomas Telford.

ST BERNARD'S WELL, DEAN VILLAGE

Next to the Water of Leith, near Stockbridge, is St Bernard's Well. According to legend, St Bernard of Clairvaux discovered the spring when visiting Scotland. Suffering from illness, he was led to it by birds and immediately felt recuperated once it touched his lips. In reality, the well was discovered in 1760 by three Heriot schoolboys who were out fishing. Believed to contain health-providing minerals, a small well house was built in the same year to mark the spot. In 1789 it was bought by Lord Gardenstone and the current structure, a Doric rotunda, was built. Underneath stands the marble statue of Hygieia, Goddess of Health, as a symbol of the water's health-giving properties.

THE DEAN GALLERY

The Dean Gallery stands in a prime position opposite the Scottish National Gallery of Modern Art, by which it is administered. Opened in 1999 to house the Paolozzi Gift of graphic art and sculpture, it now exhibits rare collections of Dada and Surrealist work and is the first new Scottish gallery dedicated to twentieth-century art. The gallery was originally an orphan hospital, but the interior has been sympathetically redesigned due to the creativity and skill of architects Terry Farrell and Partners, while the lavish exterior remains untouched.

ANN STREET, STOCKBRIDGE

This street, the most beautiful and elegant in Stockbridge, was developed by the famous painter Henry Raeburn and was named after his wife. Raeburn also worked on a number of other residential streets on the far side of the Water of Leith. Ann Street was described by the poet Sir John Betjeman as "the most attractive street in Britain". It is certainly the most unique in Edinburgh's New Town, as it is the only one to feature front gardens. Amongst those who have lived there are the publisher Robert Chambers and authors Professor John Wilson and Thomas de Quincy.

THE COLONIES, STOCKBRIDGE

To the north of Stockbridge lie the 11 parallel streets that make up the Stockbridge Colonies. Consisting of two-storey terraces, each cottage has its own entrance and private gardens. They are some of the most popular residences in this now-cosmopolitan area, but originally the houses, built by the Edinburgh Co-operative Building Company in 1861, were intended to provide low-cost housing for working people. The streets are named after the founding members of the company, such as the geologist Hugh Miller.

SCOTTISH NATIONAL GALLERY OF MODERN ART

The gallery first opened in 1960, but moved to its current location (originally the John Watson Institution) on Belford Road in 1984. With a reputation as Scotland's finest gallery of modern art, the collection has grown to incorporate 5,000 items, including paintings, sculptures, video installations and much more, with work by the likes of Matisse, Picasso, Freud, Hockney and Hirst exhibited. The grounds surrounding the gallery are also worth investigating. Sculptures by Henry Moore and Tony Cragg, among others, are on display and the front lawn has been landscaped to the design of Charles Jencks.

CORSTORPHINE CHURCH

At the eastern end of the old Corstorphine Village lies Corstorphine Church. It was built in the late fourteenth century by Sir Adam Forrester and the north transept was added in 1646, at the expense of the twelfth-century St Mary's, which was demolished to make way for it. The church was enlarged again in 1828 by William Burn because of an increasing congregation, and refurbished between 1903–05, ironically undoing much of Burn's work. Despite all these changes the church still remains impressive, with its heavy buttresses, distinctive low tower and stone slabbed roof, and has managed to maintain much of its medieval character.

ROYAL HIGHLAND SHOW

Located in Ingliston, near Edinburgh Airport, the Royal Highland Show is Scotland's (and one of the UK's) foremost showcase venues, with thousands of exhibitors and visitors attending each year in June. More than 5,000 animals – including cattle, sheep and horses – are on display in the Main Hall, as well as activities such as showjumping, sheep-shearing, heavy horse driving and farriery. The show also includes a food and drink exhibition offering the finest – primarily Scottish – delicacies. It makes for a wonderful family day out, with plenty to amuse both children and adults.

HOPETOUN HOUSE

The magnificent Hopetoun House was designed by Sir William Bruce
and built in 1669 for the Hope family, to whom it still belongs today,
in the form of the fourth Marquis of Linlithgow. In 1721 a grand
expansion was undertaken by William Adam, who remodelled the
house both outside and in, adding sweeping curves and extra
apartments to the building. The stunning architecture of this country
house is not its only appeal, however, as the house is elegantly
decorated with period furniture, tapestry and paintings as well as
wonderful ornate wooden carvings and painted ceilings.

The Falkirk Wheel

The Falkirk Wheel is the world's first and only rotating boatlift, and was opened by Queen Elizabeth II in May 2002. A magnificent, beautiful and functional structure, it is a true feat of twenty-first century engineering and is the centrepiece of the Millennium Link (a huge canal restoration project that resulted in connecting the Union Canal with the Forth and Clyde Canal). The Falkirk Wheel is also a hugely popular tourist attraction. Many are happy just to soak up the sheer glory of the 35 m (115 ft) structure, but for the more adventurous, the 'Wheel Experience' allows you to ride through the tunnel and on to the wheel itself.

FORTH RAIL BRIDGE

The more famous of the two bridges, the Forth Rail Bridge is possibly the finest bridge in Britain and is recognised all over the world. Designed by Sir Benjamin Baker and Sir John Fowler, it was built with a hefty price tag of around £3 million. The massive structure is strengthened with three cantilever towers and rises to 110 m (360 ft) above water at its highest points. The construction of the bridge took seven years, opening for use on 4 March 1890; the Prince of Wales (later King Edward VII) presided over the ceremony.

HAWES INN, SOUTH QUEENSFERRY

Situated just underneath the Forth Rail Bridge is Hawes Inn. Dating
from the seventeenth century, this inn is not only a famous drinking
institution but also a literary one. Making its first appearance in Sir
Walter Scott's *The Antiquary* when it was a coaching inn, it later
featured in Robert Louis Stevenson's *Kidnapped*. According to rumour,
Stevenson penned some of the passages of *Treasure Island* in Hawes
Inn, and in respect of the great man's work – and, of course, to serve
as a tourist attraction – the rooms of the inn have been named after
characters from his novels.

FORTH ROAD BRIDGE

The Forth Road Bridge and the Forth Rail Bridge are two of the
most beautiful architectural sights in Scotland. The road bridge is
one of the longest in the world and spans the Firth of Forth between
South and North Queensferry. The bridge was opened by the Queen
on 4 September 1964 and as well as working as a toll bridge carrying
four lanes of heavy traffic, it has gained the highest praise for its
architectural splendour and high quality of Scottish engineering.

DALMENY HOUSE

Built in 1817 by the architect William Wilkins, Dalmeny House was the first Tudor-revival house to be built in Scotland and is a striking example of neo-Gothic architecture. The interior is a Gothic feast to the eye, with its hammer-beamed hall, stained glass windows and fan-vaulted corridors all adding to the experience. One of Dalmeny's greatest attractions is the fine selection of artwork exhibited, including portraits by Gainsborough, Lawrence and Raeburn. The Napoleon Room is another treasure trove, with paintings of the great leader on display along with his furniture and trophies.

INCHCOLM ABBEY

Also known as the 'Iona of the East', Inchcolm Abbey is located on the Island of Inchcolm in the Firth of Forth, Fife. In 1235 a priory, which was founded by Alexander I in 1123, earned its status as Inchcolm Abbey. Having suffered severe attacks from the English during the fourteenth century, the abbey had to be restored and redesigned in the fifteenth century. What we see today is a romantic ruin, consisting of a thirteenth-century tower and part of the fifteenth-century abbey.

ROMAN FORT, CRAMOND

The picturesque, eighteenth-century coastal village of Cramond,
situated at the mouth of the River Almond, is home to an ancient
Roman fort. Built c. AD 142, it was used by the Romans to protect
the southern shores of the Forth and to act as a supply port for its
army. Its foundations lay undiscovered until 1954 when substantial
excavation work began and its historical importance was realised.
The most recent find, in 1997, is a Roman statue of a lioness, which
lay beneath the waters of the river for 1,800 years. It is now on display
in the National Museum of Scotland.

SNUG ANCHORAGE, CRAMOND

A thriving fishing port during the eighteenth and nineteenth centuries, Cramond harbour ceased trading after the area silted up. However, the quaint village and beautiful surrounding countryside have ensured that the harbour is still a popular place for pleasure boats to anchor. At low tide it is possible to walk out to Cramond Island, which offers stunning views across to Fife – but it is a good idea to check the tide tables before setting out so that you can be certain of being able to return to shore!

CRAMOND

The heart of the ancient village of Cramond lies to the east of the River Almond, where it flows into the Forth. Its harbour, with its splendid variety of boats and yachts, is beautifully picturesque and nestled nearby amongst the white-washed houses is the Cramond Inn, which has been serving fine food and drink since the 1870s. With its quirky layout, stunning views across the Forth and the friendly nature of the staff, this inn is a perennial attraction for tourists.

LAURISTON CASTLE

In 1926, Lauriston Castle was left to the nation by its private owners, Mr and Mrs William Robert Reid, on the condition that the property should be preserved and remain unchanged. Since that date – and fulfilling their promise – the property has been cared for by the City of Edinburgh. Built by Sir Archibald Napier, the building was originally a 1590s tower house and was extended in the Jacobean style during the 1820s by the architect William Burn. The house has had many notable Scots staying under its roof, including John Law and Thomas Allan.

ROYAL BOTANIC GARDEN

The Royal Botanic Garden was established in 1670 and is Scotland's premier garden, attracting over 660,000 visitors each year. Known locally as the 'Botanics', it is only a mile north from the heart of Edinburgh and serves as an oasis of tranquillity, as well as caring for almost 17,000 different types of plant species. The garden is also home to a world-renowned centre of botanical science, and is acknowledged as being one of the most beautiful gardens in the world.

THE GLASSHOUSE, ROYAL BOTANIC GARDEN

In the northeast corner of the Royal Botanic Garden can be found what is known as the 'Glasshouse Experience'. A remarkable 128 x 18 m (420 x 60 ft) glass structure, it is divided in to different zones, which include spectacles such as the world's largest water lily and a desert area that is dedicated to cacti and succulents. One of the most impressive features is the 21 m (70 ft) Temperate Palm House, which is the tallest in the UK and which houses myriad plants typical of sunnier climates, as well as an underground aquarium filled with tropical and coldwater fish.

NEWHAVEN FISHMARKET

Once a bustling and colourful fishing community, Newhaven was the number one oyster port in Scotland from 1572 until around 1890. During the eighteenth century, herring was the most popular and readily available fish of its day, and by the late nineteenth century a thriving fish market had developed at Newhaven Harbour. In 1994, the old fish market was redeveloped and split into three sections. The northern section remains as a fish market, the southern section houses Harry Ramsden's fish restaurant and the central section is occupied by the Newhaven Heritage Museum.

THE PORT OF LEITH

Throughout the centuries Leith has been a major port, playing a
significant role in Scottish history. Mary, Queen of Scots berthed at
Leith in 1561 to begin her role as monarch, and in the mid-seventeenth
century Cromwell settled his armies here. In fact, Leith was the
principal port of Scotland until 1707 when Glasgow took over and,
up until the 1980s, the port was the centre of Edinburgh's shipbuilding
industry. Nowadays, however, like many ports around the UK, Leith has
been developed. Property development, in the form of modern urban
flats, shops and restaurants, now provides a new form of industry.

PORTOBELLO BEACH

In its heyday, Portobello Beach attracted Edinburgh city dwellers and tourists from all over Scotland. With its open-air pool (complete with wave-making machine), marine gardens and handy train connections, Portobello was hugely popular. Sadly, all of the aforementioned attractions are now gone and it no longer draws the crowds that it used to. Nonetheless, this long, sandy beach still provides an escape from the hustle and bustle of Edinburgh, and a 'wee' paddle in the Firth of Forth when the weather is warm is just as pleasant now as it has ever been.

NEWHAILES

Built by the Scottish architect James Smith in 1686, Newhailes underwent significant changes and additions when it was purchased by Sir David Dalrymple in the early 1700s. It features one of the finest Rococo interiors in Scotland, and its extensive library was frequented by some of Scotland's most famous intellectuals during the Enlightenment. Dr Johnson claimed that it was "the most learned room in Europe". Inside, many of the original period furnishings and decorations are intact and an impressive collection of paintings, including works by John de Medina and Allan Ramsay, are on show.

TANTALLON CASTLE

Atop the cliffs of the Firth of Forth is the dramatic Tantallon Castle, near North Berwick, set against the impressive backdrop of Bass Rock. The seat of the Douglas Earls of Angus, the castle, although a noble fortification, was subject to many sieges. It was Cromwell's invasion of 1651 from which it suffered the most; the mighty castle was destroyed, leaving the ruin that remains today. In 1924, the castle passed in to the care of the State and is now preserved by Historic Scotland.

EAST LINTON PRESTON MILL

The picturesque eighteenth-century Preston Mill sits at the edge of the River Tyne, which powers its water wheel and grain-milling machinery. The conically roofed kiln and red pantile roofed buildings, together with the nearby mill pond graced with ducks and geese, create an idyll that is irresistible to the artists and photographers who gather here regularly for inspiration. The mill has not produced grain commercially since 1959, but there is an exhibition about milling that, watching and listening to the machinery in action, transports you back to the bygone days when the miller was at work.

CRAIGMILLAR CASTLE

The ruin of Craigmillar Castle dates from the mid-fifteenth century and is of great Scottish historical importance. King James V stayed at Craigmillar in 1517 and Mary, Queen of Scots rested here after the murder of her secretary David Rizzio. Moreover, it was here that the Earl of Bothwell and William Maitland schemed the downfall of the Queen's second husband, Lord Darnley. The castle was privately owned by John Gilmour from 1660, but it fell into disrepair in the eighteenth century and was given to the nation in 1946. It is now cared for by Historic Scotland.

ARTHUR'S SEAT

Located within Holyrood Park, this volcanic crag is Edinburgh's most notable natural landmark, rising to 251 m (800 ft). A series of peaks form the shape of a crouching lion, of which Arthur's Seat is the lion's head, a name by which it is also commonly known. The views from the top are outstanding, and as well as seeing the likes of Holyroodhouse, the new Scottish Parliament building and the Royal Mile, vistas as far-reaching as the River Forth and even the Trossachs are visible on a clear day.

HOLYROOD PARK

The setting of the Palace of Holyroodhouse, Holyrood Park was originally a royal hunting estate until it was enclosed by King James V around 1540. So much more than an everyday estate, Holyrood Park is an honour to its city – how many parks can boast a miniature Highland mountain or an extinct volcano? Hours can be spent exploring and taking in the pure dramatic beauty of the area. With Arthur's Seat, the wonderful Salisbury Crags, Duddingston Loch, Dunaspie Loch and St Margaret's Loch all within its boundaries, a visit is not just necessary but essential.

DUDDINGSTON LOCH, HOLYROOD PARK

One of the many beauty spots in Holyrood Park, Duddingston Loch
is overlooked by Duddingston Kirk and lies to the southwest of
Duddingston village. The reed-fringed loch, however, is not just a place
of beauty; it also functions as a bird sanctuary, and has done so since
1925. Bird watching opportunities are excellent, and for hundreds of
years it has been popular with skaters and curlers during the winter
months, when the loch freezes over. In 1778, 53 late-Bronze Age
weapons were discovered at the bottom of the loch and are now
cared for by the National Museum of Scotland.

ST MARGARET'S LOCH, HOLYROOD PARK

St Margaret's Loch is one of three in Holyrood Park. A shallow, man-made loch, its creation was ordered by Prince Albert, who wanted to further enhance the beauty of the park. With its romantic position underneath the ruins of St Anthony's Chapel, it is an atmospheric and tranquil spot that is popular with both visitors and locals. It was once a boating pond, but nowadays a significant number of geese, swans and ducks have made it their home.

SWANSTON VILLAGE

Underneath Caerketton Hill lies Swanston Village, an unusual place in that there are no shops, church, school or general facilities. The eighteenth-century, white-washed cottages that make Swanston Village so unique are the only ones in lowland Scotland that have thatched roofs made from reeds from the Firth of Tay. The cottages originally provided accommodation for farm workers at the nearby Swanston farm, and they now stand in contrast to the large number of modern, luxury houses that were built in the residential district during the 1980s and 1990s.

INDEX